· Oxford Scientific Films ·

WILDLIFE OF THE
RAINFOREST

Andrew Mitchell

**MALLARD
PRESS**

MALLARD PRESS
An Imprint of BDD Promotional Book Company, Inc.,
666 Fifth Avenue, New York, NY 10103.

Mallard Press and its accompanying design and logo
are trademarks of BDD Promotional Book Company, Inc.

CLB 2337
Copyright © 1989 Colour Library Books Ltd.
© 1989 Illustrations: Oxford Scientific Films Ltd,
Long Hanborough, England.
Color separation by Hong Kong Graphic Arts Ltd, Hong Kong.
First published in the United States of America
in 1989 by The Mallard Press.
Printed and bound in Italy by Fratelli Spada, SpA.
All rights reserved.
ISBN 0 792 45025 6

Contents

Main picture: Tall Chiapas rainforest in southern Mexico bathed in morning mist.

Inset: an orangutan high in the trees of a Sumatran rainforest.

Previous page: an eyelash viper in a Costa Rican rainforest.

1

Lungs of the Earth

There are few places in the world more mysterious and enchanting than tropical jungles. The very word conjures images of a dark place filled with tall trees, draped with looping lianas from which hooting monkeys hang, while huge, colorful butterflies and noisy birds flit between them. It might be believed that strange tribes lurk behind every bush, and that deadly snakes are poised to strike at any unsuspecting visitor. The reality is a far less frightening, but completely enchanting place.

Jungles, or to use a more accurate term, rainforests, are found in many parts of the world where the climate is warm and wet enough for them to grow. Under eight per cent of the earth's surface is covered in tropical rainforest of which almost a third is in the Brazilian Amazon. The remainder of Latin America has another quarter, West Africa just under a quarter, of which half is in Zaire, and Southeast Asia and the Pacific contain the rest. The area is decreasing by about 120 acres every minute as the trees are cut to supply the world with agricultural land and timber. Each year the environmental catastrophe this causes becomes more acute, and the first to suffer is the wildlife of the forest.

There are many kinds of rainforests, from those composed of dwarf, moss-draped trees covering the tops of cool and humid mountains, to areas where giant trees the height of a ten story building stand on sweltering, flat lowlands. Rainforests act as the lungs of the earth, producing vast amounts of oxygen for us to breathe, and absorbing potentially harmful carbon dioxide. Water evaporates into the atmosphere from the leaves, so producing great

---

Rainforests contain the richest variety of animal and plant life on earth.

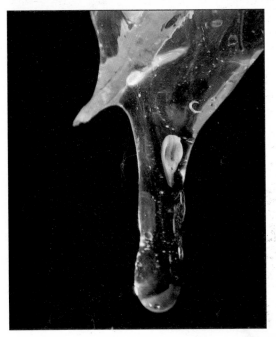

Above: a pair of glass frogs in Costa Rica guard two clutches of eggs.

Left: the humid atmosphere allows a tadpole to survive and grow inside a droplet of jelly hanging from a leaf.

storms of rain which the forest absorbs like a sponge and then slowly leaks into streams and rivers for animals to drink, fish to spawn in and humans to paddle their canoes through.

Though these forests may seem remote, we use their products every day. Many of the raw materials for such commonplace items as rubber tires, drugs, coffee, cocoa and furniture were fashioned by nature in the rainforest, where flora and fauna are interwoven into a fascinating web of life which is more intricate than any other, and which, surprisingly, involves ourselves as well.

2
Botanical Hitchhikers

It is thought that half of all life on earth lives in rainforests. There are millions of species of insects, from the largest moths to the smallest flies. Two-and-a-half acres of rainforest can support hundreds of species of trees, while a temperate woodland could boast but twenty, yet the soil is thin and they are not fertile places. The forest uses its resources very sparingly, supporting its magnificent wildlife by surviving on the sparse nutrients and minerals its soil provides, and sipping energy from the sun.

The canopy is the powerhouse of the forest. Here leaves grow from giant tree crowns, some as large as football fields, and track the sun's energy like millions of miniature solar panels. *Photosynthesis* produces sugars and the building blocks of proteins, enabling trees to grow. Their trunks may be as smooth as marble and many are as tall as 200 feet, so reaching the canopy from the ground is very difficult. Many animals which live in the canopy never visit the forest floor, and consequently little is known of their lives.

The branches of tall trees provide a home for numerous air plants, or epiphytes, such as orchids, bromeliads, mosses and *liverworts*, which can festoon the trees' branches to such an extent that their combined weight after rain causes tree limbs to crash to the ground. To survive without roots in the soil many plants have similar adaptations to desert species, a strange feature in an area where many feet of rain may fall in a year. The bromeliads of America, which are related to pineapples, have evolved water tanks by overlapping their leaves at the base to form receptacles in which enough water to fill a bucket can be stored. Mice, monkeys and various small animals use these plants as filling stations, pausing there for a drink high above the ground.

The orchids and vines create gardens of hanging flowers which bright hummingbirds or honey-eaters visit for nectar and bees buzz between. Air plants, such as huge basket ferns, help trees, too, by trapping dead leaves before they fall to the ground, so creating an airborne

Above: bromeliad epiphytes crowd the branches of a tall rainforest tree. Plants like these borrow a tree's branches to secure a place in the sun high above the dim forest floor.
Facing page: a delicate orchid in a Thailand rainforest.

It is not only flowers that are brightly colored in the forest – this bromeliad, in Chiapas, Mexico, has bright red leaves.

compost heap through which worms and beetles burrow. Amazingly, trees grow roots out of their branches to tap nutrients from this high-rise mulch, while orchids dangle their roots in space to absorb moisture from the humid air.

3
Life in the Litter

Dying vegetation falls constantly from the rainforest canopy to the dimly lit floor, providing food for countless tiny creatures which live among the leaf litter. Millipedes and woodlice prowl over the decaying leaves, which gradually rot away, leaving a fine meshwork as beautiful as any Breton lace. The nutrients locked up in leaves are vital to the forest's survival, and can quickly be washed away in a deluge of rainwater. Fortunately, fungal threads grow rapidly around decomposing leaves and transfer their goodness to tree roots. These vital fungi are seldom seen except when they grow beautiful spooring bodies above the leaves, and some of them are luminous, casting a strange, eerie glow over the floor of the forest at night.

Above: fungi help to rot the litter of fallen leaves, thus releasing nutrients for trees and other growing plants to use.

Right: a tamandua searches for termites and ants among the leaves of the forest.

The miniature jungle of fallen leaves is a fertile hunting ground for the crowned litter snake.

Ants scurry over the forest floor, scavenging carcasses of dead insects that have fallen from the canopy above and carrying them to their nests. Army ants are among the most terrifying scavengers, moving in swarms of hundreds of thousands, butchering any small creature in their path. Their jaws are so strong that Indians use them to close open wounds in their skin, twisting off the ant's head and so locking the mandibles in position. A swarm of army ants flushes many insects from their hiding places among the leaves, and creatures such as the antbird and predatory flies follow them, hoping for an easy meal.

Giant anteaters steer clear of army ants, but use their powerful claws to tear open the nests of other species, which they gather up with their long, sticky tongues. The South American tamandua's black and brown coat color provides effective camouflage in the forest, where it specializes in eating termites as well as ants, which they lick from rotting wood on the ground and from nests in the branches. In Asia and Africa, the *pangolin* occupies a similar niche in the forest. The giant African pangolin may consume as many as 200,000 ants in a night. With their shambling gait and curious, scale-covered bodies they resemble "perambulating artichokes".

Many creatures forage in the leaf litter not for insects but for nuts and fruits which have fallen from the branches. Wild pigs of Asia and Africa, and *peccaries* and pacas of South America, crack and gnaw nuts, but many are buried and forgotten and will later grow into trees.

4

Clingers and Leapers

To the animals the rainforest is not just a tangle of tree limbs, but a network of vertical tracks and arboreal highways which are as familiar to them as any favorite walk is to us. Animals need to move in search of food, mates and safe shelter, and have adapted themselves to meet the challenges the forest offers by clinging, leaping and even flying.

In the region of vertical tree trunks beneath the canopy, creatures such as tarsiers and Madagascar's unique lemurs use their powerful back legs to launch themselves on prodigious jumps between the trunks. Tarsiers have huge eyes which enable them to search in the dark for large insects, while small pads on their fingers help them to grip. Tree frogs also have such adhesive pads, though they rarely leap among the branches, preferring to clamber gently over leaves.

Many monkeys have evolved an ability to clamber through the branches with remarkable skill. Those of South America use their prehensile tails as a fifth hand, enabling them to hang from the branches, keeping their hands free to grasp otherwise inaccessible fruits and leaves. Monkeys of Africa and Asia never evolved such tails, but gibbons manage superbly by swinging hand over hand beneath branches, flinging themselves as much as ten yards through the air to land safely in another tree. They are the fastest primates in the forest.

Surprisingly, tree architecture varies in different localities, and animals have had to adapt to meet open or closed canopies. Tree

---

A howler monkey sets out on a highway through the tree tops.

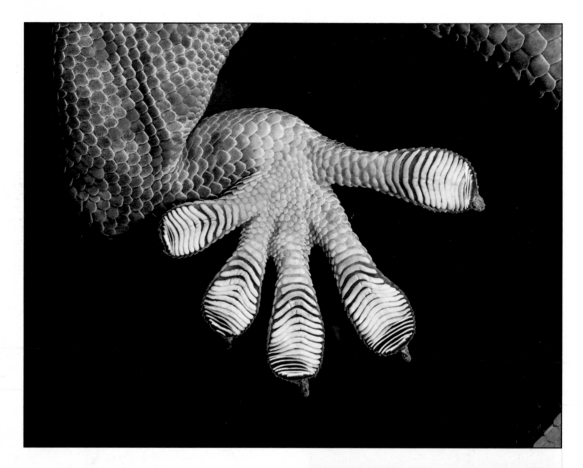

Tiny hooks in the ridges on the underside of this Tokay gecko's foot allow it to cling to almost any surface.

crowns do not interlock, but have a gap of about a yard between them. To cross from tree to tree presents smaller animals with a problem. Small squirrels rush along branches and hurl themselves into space, clutching at branches lower down as they fall. A safer method is to glide. Employing the evolutionary adaptation of a cloak of skin streched between fore- and hindlimb, sugar gliders can move with ease between trees to search for nectar and sweet sap, and the larger flying lemurs can float right across a valley. The flying lizard deploys two skin wings by streching out its ribs, and there are even snakes which glide, and frogs which use parachutes of skin between their toes.

Above: the silky anteater has an opposable claw and pad to grip the branches, as well as a prehensile tail.

Facing page: tree frogs, such as this red-eyed frog, with their long, padded toes, are masters at creeping around the rainforest.

5

Flowers and their Friends

At certain times of the year pink, yellow or purple flowers burst from the tree crowns and the vines threading between them, splashing the leaves with bright colors. The purpose of these flowers is to attract insects, birds and even bats as pollen distributors. Pollen must be transferred from flower to flower for fertilization to occur, and while some plants use the wind, in the rainforest a personal pollen carrier is more reliable.

Right: freed from the orchid trap with a pollen packet glued to its back, this bee is ready to become the unwitting pollinator of the next bucket orchid it visits.

Above: a spider monkey takes a drink from a balsa flower, and so may help to disperse its pollen.

Facing page bottom: a long-tailed hermit hummingbird visits a passionflower for nectar and receives a dusting of pollen.

To attract a pollinator a flower must be conspicuous and provide a reward. Often this is nectar, though many offer pollen and some nothing at all, merely deceiving a visiting insect into thinking a reward is in store. *Swartzia panamensis* in Central America attracts many bees to its strings of yellow flowers, where they receive a gift of pollen. Swartzia trees are often far apart in the forest and only the largest of the many bee species that visit the flowers is powerful enough to make the journey regularly between them, so only it is likely to be the true pollinator. The remainder are merely robbers.

Birds see red clearly, so flowers designed to attract them are often of that color. *Brownea's* spiky red flowers have long stamens which dust a visiting hummingbird's feathers with pollen, which will be deposited on the next *Brownea* flower the bird visits. Passionflower vines are also favorites with hummingbirds, whose long beaks probe deeply for the nectar concealed within the huge flowers. The deepest-probing pollinator must be the moth *Xanthopan morgani praedicta,* which has a proboscis of ten inches to match the tube-like flowers it feeds on. Both moth and flower have evolved together, so that only this moth can *pollinate* it. The moth gets an assured food supply, the plant a perfect pollinator.

Even more incredible is the behavior of bees attracted to bucket orchids. Just before dawn the flowers open and drip fluid into a small, thimble-shaped container. A bee attracted to the flowers will slip on the oily surface and sink into the fluid. Its only means of escape is a small tunnel, through which it crawls. There the plant traps it while a pollen packet is glued to its back. This the bee will unwittingly pass on to the next bucket orchid it visits.

6

A Feast of Fruit

Why do many rainforest trees produce such huge quantities of fruit? The answer is that they need their offspring carried far and wide to good germination sites. The balsawood tree produces fruiting bodies that resemble furry rabbits' feet, and disperses its seed, attached to wispy hairs, on air currents. The kapok tree does the same, its fluffy seed masses also making excellent stuffing for mattresses. Being a fast-growing pioneer species, the balsawood tree can take advantage of light winds in open parts of the forest, but in the jungle canopy there is little wind, so trees encourage animals to help scatter their seeds.

Most of the fruits that we eat are larger and more fleshy than those that grow in the rainforests. Trees produce three kinds of fruits to attract monkeys, birds and other animals to eat them. Some are grape-sized with lots of small seeds, such as figs. A pigeon may eat these and, while many seeds will be destroyed in its *gizzard*, some will pass through and perhaps germinate. Fig trees start life as epiphytes growing from such a seed dropped onto a tree branch.

Fruit that falls to the ground is not wasted, but provides a feast for many animals, including these cotton-stainer bugs.

Above: a white-fronted parrot feasting on fruit in a Costa Rican canopy.

Top: the bright red fruits of the lipstick tree attract birds and Indians too, who use the red dye to decorate themselves.

They send roots all the way to the ground, and these eventually encase and kill the host tree, by which time the strangling fig can stand on its own. Fig fruits appeal to opportunistic species such as hornbills, toucans and gibbons, which take a little bit of everything rather than specializing in one or two fruit types.

Another strategy employed by trees is to provide a complete diet in the form of a nutritious fruit encasing a large seed. An avocado is a good example. The ample, oily flesh of such seeds buys the attendance of larger dispersers, which come to depend on them for food. Creatures such as the orang-utan enjoy eating these items in the rainforest feast. Producing such a big fruit is expensive for a tree, so to make sure they are not wasted, many cover their seeds in thin, bright coatings called arils. These are red to attract birds which favor the protein-rich *aril* and can manage the large seeds it covers. The seed is protected by a hard coating and so is not damaged by a bird's gizzard, and will eventually fall into the forest, perhaps to germinate.

7

Hunters

There are many hunters that prowl the forest at night. In the Amazon rainforest the jaguar is king, while in Africa and Asia the similar-looking leopard patrols the forest in search of small antelope to pounce upon. Black panthers creep stealthily there also, but they are merely leopards with a darkened coat. The most tree-loving of the big cats is the clouded leopard of Borneo, which climbs skilfully among the branches and is capable of swatting pigeons out of the air with its huge, spoon-shaped paws.

Smaller spotted cats such as the ocelot and the fox-like linsang are masters of stealth, and creep along branches high above the ground to snatch roosting birds or chicks from their nests. Many of these cats are hunted for their skins and so are becoming rare. Most feared of all is the powerful tiger, capable of bringing down the largest deer in the rainforest. Only those that are injured and lose their hunting skills, are likely to become man-eaters. Some mammals such as anteaters only hunt ants or termites, while the potto prefers poisonous caterpillars, grasping them with its hands and rubbing off their toxic hairs before popping them into its mouth.

For a bird of prey to chase its intended victim through the forest requires supreme flying skill. The harpy eagle is the most powerful eagle in the world and, despite its huge size, can fly

Facing page: jaguars will climb rainforest trees in search of prey.

Above: the harpy eagle tears flesh with its supremely powerful beak and talons.

beneath the tree crowns, rising upward to snatch an unsuspecting sloth clinging under a branch. Almost nothing is known about the habits of forest-living *raptors*, but it has been discovered that *Micrastaur* falcons hunt in a most peculiar way. They hide under bushes crying "eek-eek" to give their position away, then fly out to snatch inquisitive birds which are attracted by the noise.

Everyone is afraid of snakes in the rainforest, though they are rarely seen. Giant pythons of Sulawesi in Indonesia have been known to swallow humans whole, and the anaconda of South America could do the same, but the chances of it doing so are remote. Green tree pythons seek out their prey using the heat-sensitive pits in their snouts, and blunt-headed tree snakes have special spines which enable them to stretch across gaps in between branches and snatch small lizards sleeping on leaves.

A harlequin frog falls prey to a fire-bellied snake.

8
Sending a Message

This vine snake looks terrifying, but is harmless. Its display is a bluff.

Above: poisonous frogs advertize their distastefulness with bright colors.

Facing page top: many caterpillars are beautifully camouflaged to avoid being seen among the leaves on which they feed. This hawkmoth has a defense trick. Should danger threaten, it raises itself up into a startle display.

Facing page bottom: a tree frog's call may attract a female, but warn off a rival male.

The rainforest is so thick with trees and bushes that it is very easy to get lost and very hard to be seen. To stay in touch with a mate, to signal the location of a food source, or to tell others to keep away, animals have evolved remarkable methods of communication involving color, scent and sound.

Certain frequencies of sound will travel further than others in the forest. Amazingly, these very frequencies, or "sound windows", are used by many monkeys and birds to project their calls. Low frequency, resonating calls work best in the understorey, so birds such as the curasow of the Amazon and the huge, flightless cassowaries in New Guinea's forests have booming calls. Birds that live higher up in the branches can afford to use higher frequency twittering calls which carry more information. The blue wattled bell bird has a very powerful call sounding like the clang of a heavy metal hammer hitting a blacksmith's anvil. Birds with these kinds of calls are known as anvil birds.

There are loud monkeys too. Howler monkeys sound like roaring leopards, and the gray-cheeked mangabey's call resembles the gobble of a turkey. Most tuneful of all primates are the gibbons, and the males and females sing together in distinctive duets which echo across

the forest as the mists of dawn are rising from the trees. *Cicadas* are the noisiest of the insects. Their larvae may live for fifteen years under the soil before they climb into the trees, where they emerge as adults and sing their piercing call to attract a mate before they die a matter of weeks later.

Many animals join this dawn chorus, from rasping insects to melodious birds. This helps them to establish territories and attract possible mates at the beginning of the day. Color is an equally useful method of getting a message across. Toucans have brightly colored beaks which they can use like a flag in the tree tops, perhaps to attract other birds into the feeding tree. Butterflies and moths use their wings both to camouflage themselves and to attract mates with bright colors. They also use strong scents which can be wafted through the forest from tiny hair pencils in their abdomens. Males can be attracted from over a mile away.

9

Things that Come out at Night

Night comes suddenly in the rainforest. As twilight turns rapidly to darkness, the forest changes its tune. Numerous cicadas might begin to call like a symphony of miniature chain saws. You can almost set your watch by their timekeeping. Frogs, too, of all shapes and sizes, emerge to sit on rocks beside streams, their rounded throat sacks bulging almost to bursting point. As they boom and peep to attract their mates and establish territories, their calls change as the night progresses. The male coqui frog starts with a "ko" call to repel males, then after about an hour this changes to a "ko-kee". Only then will a female creep up to look him over.

It is not always frogs that are attracted to these sounds. A bat species in Central America listens to all the calls of male frogs and swoops in on them with deadly skill, snatching the little amphibians from stream banks in total darkness. Male katydids, large grasshopper-like insects, also call loudly at night and attract bats specializing in searching for nocturnal insects lurking on the leaves. To avoid being eaten the

---

Some fruit bats forage at night for nectar and pollen.

The tarsier's huge eyes help it to find food at night.

katydids call only in short bursts, so that the patrolling bats have no time to home in on them. Many bats are not blind but prefer to use sonar to find their way around. By listening to echoes from their high frequency calls they can build up a sound picture of their surroundings, perhaps in a similar way to ultra-sound, which can "see" babies inside a mother's womb. Listening to the echoes returning from a moth's body, a tiny, *insectivorous* bat can scoop it out of the air with its wing or tail. Flying foxes leave their roosts and flap lazily, on wings over a yard across, over the forest at night in search of fruiting trees. These huge bats, found from West Africa to the central Pacific islands, use their well-developed eyes and have poor sonar capabilities.

Night is a time of great mystery in the forest; the bushes move and leaves rustle, but the creatures that cause them to do so rarely give themselves away. Was it a leopard, a small civet cat, a snake or just a monkey high in the branches scratching himself to sleep? You may never know.

10
War on Leaves

All trees need their leaves to capture energy from the sun. Having them ruined by millions of voracious caterpillars, or troops of hungry monkeys, lessens a tree's chance of survival and opens wounds for bacteria and fungi to infect.

Because many tropical leaves are so hard to digest, mammals need a large stomach enriched with powerful bacteria to break down the leaf matter. Many leaf-eating monkeys are in effect walking compost heaps, but they cannot rely on leaves alone and must supplement their diet with a little fruit and the occasional insect for protein. Iguanas climb into the treetops in South America to eat leaves and warm themselves in the sun, so speeding the otherwise-slow digestion process. The three-toed sloth conserves the poor energy available in leaves by hardly moving at all, spending eighteen hours of every day

hanging motionless beneath a chosen tree branch, camouflaged from would-be predators by green algae growing in special grooves in its hairs, which helps it to blend with its surroundings. Their slothful life is efficient and they are one of the most common animals in the rainforest canopy, though they are rarely seen by humans.

Insects eat almost twelve per cent of all leaf material that a tree produces. To keep this consumption to a minimum, trees infuse their leaves with poisons such as caffeine, terpene, morphine and tannin as well as sticky latex, which gums up insects' jaws. Certain of these chemicals have become the precursors for anti-

Pierid butterfly eggs sit like time bombs waiting to hatch hungry caterpillars.

cancer drugs, and even the contraceptive pill. Although these poisons prevent a wide range of insects from attacking leaves, in this botanical war there are always specialists who manage to find a way through a plant's defenses. Leaf-cutting ants do so by getting help from fungi. They chop small pieces of leaf, even from the highest branches, and carry them down to their nests beneath the ground. In subterranean chambers they seed the decaying leaves with fungal spores, which break down the tough leaves for them, leaving the ants to feed on the growing mushrooms. The exhausted leaf material is then gathered up by worker ants who carry it outside the nest and drop it in neat, conical piles some distance away.

Left: a red howler monkey feeding on leaves in Venezuela.
Below: a mother and baby sloth hanging in the branches.

11
A Home in the Trees

Giving birth and raising young in the branches of the rainforest is a precarious business. Gibbons live in small family groups comprising an adult male, a female and one or two offspring. They remain as a family unit until the youngsters grow old enough to leave. Other monkeys live in larger groups with looser family ties. Most primates do not make fine nests like birds, but many other mammals do. Tiny possums, squirrels and mice nest in small tree holes which they line with fur and moss.

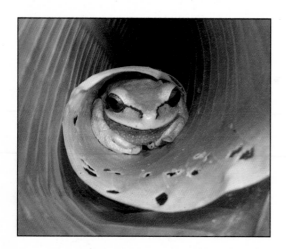

An unfurling leaf provides sleeping quarters for a masked puddle frog.

Tree holes are premium apartments for many animals who prefer to live above ground. Often they are first made by woodpeckers who have broken through to a tree's hollow interior in search of grubs. In South America a quetzal may follow and use the site as a nest. In Asia the hornbill cock bird seals the hen inside a tree hole by plastering mud over the entrance, leaving only enough room for the scimitar-like beak to protrude. Inside, safe from predators which cannot get past her sharp beak, she loses her feathers, which then form nesting material, incubates her eggs and rears her brood, all the time being fed by the male. When the young are fledged, the male releases them from their prison

Tent bats roosting under a heliconia leaf.

A female arrow poison frog carrying her tadpoles to a tree top nursery.

to fly over the forest. *Bromeliad epiphytes* of the American rainforests save water by trapping rain in the base of their leaves. Many small animals pause there to drink, and mosquitos and giant damsel flies use these miniature water tanks as nursery grounds for their larvae. The *marsupial* frog carries its eggs beneath flaps of skin on its back, releasing the newly-hatched tadpoles into a bromeliad when they are mature. Oddest of all are tiny, ground-living arrow poison frogs, so named for their toxic skin secretions which Indians use to tip their arrows. These small frogs carry their tadpoles piggy-back style into the branches and place them secretly into a bromeliad, where they grow safe from fish and shrimps which might attack them in streams. Should one run out of mosquito larvae to eat, the female frog returns each day to deliver a single unfertilized egg; a small daily food parcel to keep her tadpole going .

12
Remarkable Partnerships

In the rainforest the climate is equable and food is often plentiful, but competition for resources is keen. Evolution has favored the formation of partnerships between animal species or between plants and animals which at times seem extraordinarily complex.

Kingfishers and pygmy parrots will often lay their eggs inside termite nests, which provide a warm, humid *incubation* chamber. Surprisingly, the termites do no harm, but attack marauding predators after the bird's chicks. Oropendola birds prefer to hang their basket-like nests in trees infested with trigonid bee colonies. The bees chase off botflies which try to lay eggs on the newly hatched oropendola chicks, and whose maggots would kill them. The cowbird lays its eggs in oropendola nests, but they are usually ejected, except when there are no bees sharing the tree. Then the oropendolas raise the cowbird chick as one of their own because it hatches first and picks off any botfly maggots that later appear on the oropendola's own chicks. Thus the cowbird acts as a protector where bees are not present, and the oropendolas tolerate it.

Plants often have a special relationship with ants. Many plants feed ants with nectar from special pores outside their flowers, in return for which the ants protect their food source from

Above: an oropendola arriving at its nest.

Facing page: ants feeding on beltian bodies provided for them by an acacia tree.

destructive caterpillars. Some acacia trees go further and provide small, protein-filled capsules called beltian bodies, clustered like miniature jugglers' clubs on leafy twigs, which are essential to the ant's diet. The ants, which live in complex communities inside the tree's hollow thorns, rush out and attack anything that may harm the tree.

Hydnophytum is shaped like a football-sized prickly hedgehog with leaves coming out of its nose. It grows on the trunks or branches of trees in Southeast Asia. Minute *Iridomyrmex* ants live inside small purple chambers within the plant, and each night stream down onto the forest floor to gather insect carcasses that have fallen from the canopy. They return these to tiny graveyards inside the plant and grow fungi on them. The fungi rot the insect bodies, releasing nutritious juices which the plant absorbs through warty internal roots. The ants feed on the fungi, the plants get a source of nitrogen, the ants a home.

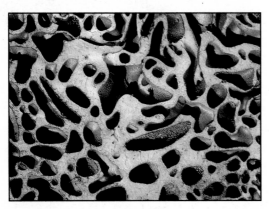

Natural chambers within the hydnophytum stem are used by the ants to raise their young and bury their dead.

13
Dangers to Rainforest Wildlife

More than predation by jungle cats, birds of prey, snakes and disease, human beings present the single greatest danger to animals of the rainforest and, indeed, to the rainforest itself. Tribal people who have learned to live with the forest have developed great hunting skills, using blowpipes or poisoned arrows, and traps. Most animals, such as monkeys and pigeons in the trees, or pigs and deer on the ground, are hunted for food. The Punan of Borneo use poison steamed from the bark of the ipoh tree to tip their darts, while the Waorani of the Amazon use toxin from the skin of poison arrow frogs. A darted monkey dies quickly and, because the poison makes muscles relax, it falls to the ground to provide a meal for the hunter's family.

Today, the introduction of firearms has tipped the balance more firmly in the hunter's favor, and many animals are vanishing from the forests where they once lived. Many monkeys are killed and their attractive skins are sold to tourists; rare and beautiful parrots are snared in the wild to sell to collectors abroad. Crocodile farming is now becoming big business in countries like New Guinea, to supply the world with fine leather for shoes and handbags, which, in fact, reduces the need to capture crocodiles from rivers and lakes.

A wild proboscis monkey from the Borneo is here enslaved as a pet.

As countries in which these magnificent rainforests grow build hospitals, ports and roads, their trees are logged to provide foreign exchange to finance the development process. Then, pioneer farmers grow crops for a few years where rich and thriving rainforest once stood, to feed their rapidly growing families. Often, useless, infertile scrubland results. Neither the wildlife nor the tribal people of the forest can survive such an onslaught, and its consequences may affect us all through world climatic change.

The wildlife of the rainforest has given us much of value. Rubber, coffee, cocoa, even cornflakes came from rainforest plants. Who could imagine a world without gentle gorillas, prowling panthers or mischievious marmosets?

All over the world man is destroying the rainforest faster than ever before. No one knows the effect this will have on our planet.

Yet many of these creatures are now severely endangered. Fortunately, there is a mood of change in the world, with greater thought being given to the protection of wildlife and the environment than ever before. Many people now refuse to buy products whose manufacture might endanger wildlife, and new efforts are being made to find ways of replanting rainforests. Half of all the life on earth exists in rainforests, and we cannot afford to lose it.

Glossary

ARIL Thin, red protein coat around a seed provided to attract birds to eat them.

BROMELIAD Epiphyte related to pineapples, with serrated leaves which trap rain water. Popular in homes and offices for their red flowers and internal pools of water.

BROWNEA Small tree in shrub layer of the forest producing red spiky flowers.

CICADA Large, flying bug, famous in rainforests for its very loud call, especially at dawn and dusk.

EPIPHYTE Plant which grows on another plant. Rainforest trees are often covered in them, from tiny mosses to large ferns.

GIZZARD A bird's secondary stomach, used for grinding food.

INCUBATION Process through which a bird hatches its eggs by sitting on them to keep them warm.

INSECTIVORE Animal that specializes in eating insects.

LIVERWORT Lichen-like plant with liver shaped leaves.

MARSUPIAL Animal which rears its young in a pouch.

PANGOLIN Mammal of West African and Asian rainforests specializing in eating termites or ants. Has a prehensile tail and is covered in horny scales.

PECCARY Medium-sized, hairy pig-like creature found in Central American rainforests.

PHOTOSYNTHESIS Chemical process by which plants convert the sun's energy to sugar.

POLLINATION Process by which genetic material inside pollen grains is transferred from one flower to another leading to fertilization.

RAPTOR Day-flying bird of prey.

SWARTZIA Medium-height tree of the American tropics belonging to the pea family.

TAMANDUA Arboreal anteater found in Central American rainforest.